Here's How

PAINTING

29 Projects with Paint

Creative Publishing
international

MINNEAPOLIS, MINNESOTA

Contents

Introduction

You may think that painting walls is such an obvious skill that you have no need for a book on the subject. But do you know the difference between eggshell enamel and gloss enamel, and when to use each? Are you aware of the proper painting sequence for elaborate paneled cabinets? Do you know what a faux serpentine paint finish is, and how to achieve it? And have you mastered the skill of mimicking textured plaster finishes with ordinary paint?

If not, then this ingenious, inexpensive book is for you. For much less than the cost of a good paintbrush, you'll learn a remarkable amount of basic painting information, as well as detailed instructions for creating 18 specialty finishes, from color washes to pickled paint finishes for a classic antique look.

The book opens with some basics on paint chemistry and the tools and materials you'll need for painting walls, woodwork and furniture. You'll also learn about some of the specialty tools that now make painting easier and quicker, including power rollers, airless sprayers, and paint additives. Next, you'll get a refresher course on basic application techniques with brushes and rollers. You may think you already know this, but have a look; you'll be surprised by insights that will help you get truly professional results.

The heart of the book, though, is the central section, where you'll discover the detailed recipes for painting specific surfaces, as well as for achieving all the most popular specialty finishes. These are finishes that are often presented in specialty seminars at paint stores and home centers, but here, for less than $10, you'll get no-fail instructions for successfully creating all of them. And of course you'll also learn how to clean up your work site and tools.

Here's How: Painting is a remarkable bargain. For the cost of a good magazine, you now have a solid instructional manual for virtually any painting project you want to tackle.

1. Paint Selection

Paints are either water-base (latex) or alkyd-base. Latex paint is easy to apply and clean up, and the improved chemistry of today's latexes makes them suitable for nearly every application. Some painters feel that alkyd paint allows for a smoother finished surface, but local regulations may restrict the use of alkyd-base products.

Paints come in various sheens. Paint finishes range from flat to high-gloss enamels. Gloss enamels dry to a shiny finish, and are used for surfaces that need to be washed often, like walls in bathrooms and kitchens, and for woodwork. Flat paints are used for most wall and ceiling applications.

Paint prices typically are an accurate reflection of quality. As a general rule, buy the best paint your budget can afford. High-quality paints are easier to use and they look better than cheaper paints. And because quality paints last longer and cover better than budget paints, often requiring fewer coats, they are usually less expensive in the long run.

Always use a good primer to coat surfaces before painting. The primer bonds well to all surfaces and provides a durable base that helps keep the finish coat from cracking or peeling. When using deep colors, choose a tinted primer to reduce the number of coats of paint necessary to achieve good coverage.

How to Estimate Paint ▶

1) Length of wall or ceiling (feet)	
2) Height of wall, or width of ceiling	×
3) Surface area	=
4) Coverage per gallon of chosen paint	÷
5) Gallons of paint needed	=

How to Select a Quality Paint

Paint coverage (listed on can labels) of quality paint should be about 400 square feet per gallon. Bargain paints (left) may require two or even three coats to cover the same area as quality paints.

High washability is a feature of quality paint. The pigments in bargain paints (right) may "chalk" and wash away with mild scrubbing.

Paint Sheens ▶

Paint comes in a variety of surface finishes, or sheens. Gloss enamel (A) provides a highly reflective finish for areas where high washability is important. All gloss paints tend to show surface flaws. Alkyd-base enamels have the highest gloss. Medium-gloss latex enamel creates a highly washable surface with a slightly less reflective finish.

Like gloss enamels, medium-gloss paints (B) tend to show surface flaws. Eggshell enamel (C) combines the soft finish with the washability of enamel. Flat latex (D) is an all-purpose paint with a soft finish that hides surface irregularities.

2. Tools & Equipment

Most painting jobs can be done with a few quality tools. Purchase two or three premium brushes, a sturdy paint pan that can be attached to a stepladder, a supply of disposable pan liners, and a variety of roller covers. With proper care, high-quality brushes will last for years.

Brushes made of hog or ox bristles should be used only with alkyd-base paints. All-purpose brushes blend polyester, nylon, and sometimes animal bristles. Choose a straight-edged 3" wall brush, a 2" straight-edged trim brush, and a tapered sash brush.

How to Choose a Paintbrush

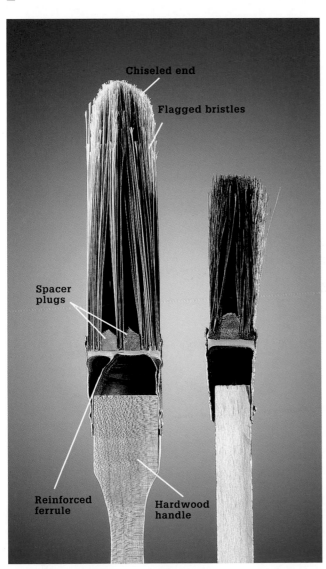

Chiseled end

Flagged bristles

Spacer plugs

Reinforced ferrule

Hardwood handle

A quality brush (left), has a shaped hardwood handle and a sturdy reinforced ferrule made of noncorrosive metal. Multiple spacer plugs separate the bristles. A quality brush has flagged (split) bristles and a chiseled end for precise edging. A cheaper brush (right) will have a blunt end, unflagged bristles, and a cardboard spacer plug that may soften when wet.

A 3" straight-edged brush (top) is a good choice for cutting paint lines at ceilings and in corners. For painting woodwork, a 2" trim brush (middle) works well. Choose brushes with chiseled tips for painting in corners. A tapered sash brush (bottom) can help when painting corners on window sashes.

3. Paint Rollers & Roller Accessories

A good roller frame is an inexpensive, time-saving tool that can last for years. Choose a well-balanced frame with nylon bearings and a comfortable handle with a threaded end that accepts an extension handle.

Roller covers are available in a wide variety of materials and nap lengths. Most jobs can be done with ⅜" nap. Select medium-priced synthetic roller covers that can be reused a few times before being discarded. Bargain roller covers might shed fibers onto the painted surface, and cannot be cleaned or reused. Rinse all roller covers before use to remove lint.

Use more expensive lamb's wool roller covers when using most alkyd-based paints. Mohair covers work well with gloss alkyd paints, where complete smoothness is important.

Synthetic covers (left) are good with most paints, especially latexes. Wool or mohair roller covers (right) give an even finish with alkyd products. Choose good-quality roller covers, which will be less likely to shed lint.

Select the proper roller cover for the surface you intend to paint. A ¼"-nap cover is used for very flat surfaces. A ⅜"-nap cover will cover the small flaws found in most flat walls and ceilings. A 1"-nap cover fills spaces in rough surfaces, such as concrete blocks or stucco walls. Foam rollers fit into small spaces and work well when painting furniture or doing touch-ups. Corner rollers have nap on the ends and make it easy to paint corners without cutting in the edges.

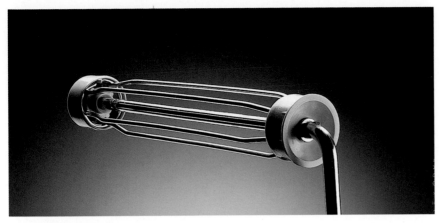

Choose a sturdy roller with a wire cage construction. Nylon bearings should roll smoothly and easily when you spin the cage. The handle end should be threaded for attaching an extension handle.

Buy a paint tray with legs that allow the tray to sit steadily on the shelf of a ladder. Disposable tray liners simplify clean up: simply allow the paint to dry completely and throw the liner away in the regular trash. Look for a textured ramp that keeps the roller turning easily.

A five-gallon paint container and paint screen speed up the process of painting large areas. Some manufacturers offer containers with built-in roller trays that let you paint straight from the container. Do not try to balance a five-gallon container on the shelf of a ladder—it's too heavy.

Use an adjustable extension handle to paint ceilings and tall walls easily without a ladder.

4. Specialty Painting Tools

Surfaces with unusual angles and contours are sometimes difficult to paint with standard rollers and brushes. Specialty tools make some painting situations easier. Disposable foam brushes, for instance, are excellent for applying an even coat of clear varnish to smooth woodwork, and paint gloves make painting contoured surfaces a much simpler task.

An airless paint sprayer is useful for painting large areas or for irregular surfaces, like louvered closet doors. All sprayers produce some overspray, so wear protective gear and mask off all areas likely to be splattered. Movable workpieces should be painted outside or in your basement or garage. Thinning the paint before spraying will result in easier use of the tool and more even coverage.

Specialty roller covers, available in a variety of light and heavy textures, make it easy to achieve a consistent, textured surface.

A bendable tool can be shaped to fit unusual surfaces, such as window shutters or the fins of cast-iron radiators.

A paint glove simplifies painting of pipes and other contoured surfaces, like wrought iron.

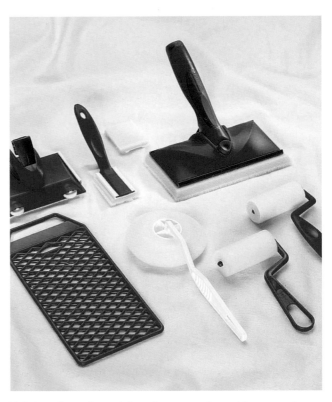

Paint pads and specialty rollers come in a wide range of sizes and shapes to fit different painting needs.

Aerosol spray paint speeds the painting of any small, intricate jobs, like heat registers.

A paint mixer bit attaches to a power drill to stir paints quickly and easily. Use a variable-speed drill at low speed to avoid air bubbles in the paint.

C

D

G

I

H

J

B

A

K

E

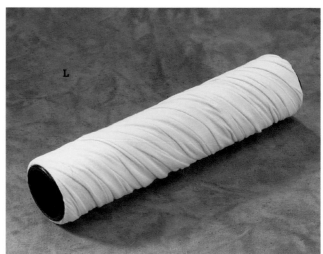

L

5. Advanced Painting Tools

Many tools and paintbrushes have been developed for creating specialized decorative painting effects. Depending on how they are used, some tools may create more than one effect. Working with the various tools and learning their capabilities is an important step in becoming a successful faux finisher. Most tools and paintbrushes are available in a range of sizes. As a general rule, use the largest size tool or brush suitable for the surface area.

Some tools and brushes are designed for manipulating the wet glaze on the surface. These include: floggers (A), blending brushes or softeners (B), stipplers (C), and a mottler (D). Also helpful is a dual Woolie (E) roller and an edging tool (F).

Certain faux effects are achieved using removal tools, such as a wood graining rocker (G), overgrainers (H), wipe-out tools (I), and combs (J). Artist's erasers (K) can be notched and used as combs (page 69). Rag rollers (L) are also available for faux effects.

Specialty brushes designed for applying paints and glazes include artist's brushes, such as rounds (M), liners (N), or a dagger (O). These may be used for veining in marble finishes or graining in wood finishes. Stenciling brushes (P) are available in ¼" to 1¼" diameters. Other tools, such as a sea sponge (Q) or feathers (R) are also used for applying paints and glazes. A check roller (S) is a specialty tool used for applying pore structure in a faux oak finish.

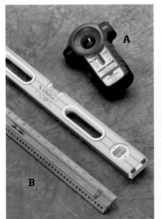

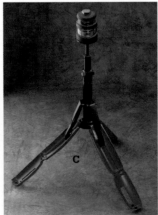

Many advanced painting designs require straight, level lines. A bubblestick (A) or carpenter's level (B) will work well. Laser levels (C) make quick work of creating perfectly straight, level lines.

6. Advanced Painting Materials

Latex and acrylic paints can be used successfully for a wide range of faux finishes and techniques. Because they are water-based, they are easy to clean up with just soap and water, and they are also safer for the environment than oil-based paints.

Water-based paints dry quickly, which is not necessarily an advantage in decorative painting, especially for techniques that require some manipulation of the paint on the surface. To increase open time, or the length of time the paint can be manipulated, several paint additives have been developed. These include latex paint conditioner, such as Floetrol, and acrylic paint extender. These products are available at paint retailers and craft supply stores.

For some decorative painting techniques, it is preferable to use a paint glaze, which is usually thinner and more translucent than paint. There are some premixed acrylic paint glazes available in limited colors. These may be mixed to produce additional glaze colors. Untinted acrylic mediums in gloss, satin, or matte finishes also are available for mixing with acrylic or latex paint to make glazes. The glaze medium does not change the color of the paint; generally a small amount of paint is added to the glaze medium, just enough to give it the desired color. Latex or acrylic paint can also be mixed with water-based urethane or varnish for a very translucent glaze.

Tips for Using Paint Glazes

- Protect the surrounding area with a drop cloth or plastic sheet, and wear old clothing because working with a glaze can be messy.
- Use a wide painter's tape to mask off the surrounding surfaces. Firmly rub the edges of the tape to ensure that the glaze will not seep under it.
- Use a paint roller to apply the glaze when even coverage is desired or when painting a large surface, such as a wall.
- Use a paintbrush to apply the glaze when smooth finish is desired, or when painting a small item.
- Use a sponge applicator to apply the glaze when more variation and pattern in the surface is desired, or when painting a small item.
- Manipulate glaze while it is still wet. Although humidity affects the setting time, the glaze can usually be manipulated for a few minutes.
- Work with an assistant when using glaze on a large surface. While one person applies the glaze, the other can manipulate it.

Low-luster latex enamel paint is used for the base coat under faux finishes. The slightly sheened surface gives the finish a base to cling to, while allowing manipulation tools to move easily on the surface.

Acrylic paints are available in a wide range of colors. They can be used alone for stenciling, or mixed with acrylic mediums to create glazes for decorative paint finishes.

Premixed acrylic paint glazes are available in a variety of colors for faux finishing. They are slightly translucent and contain additives for extended open time.

Acrylic mediums, or glaze mediums, can be mixed with acrylic or latex paint to create paint glazes with gloss, satin, or matte finishes.

Mix paint together (called "boxing") in a large pail to eliminate slight color variations between cans. Stir the paint thoroughly with a wooden stick or power drill attachment. To keep paint from building up in the groove around the paint can lid, pound several small nail holes into the groove. This allows the paint to drip back into the can.

7. Basic Painting Methods

For a professional-looking paint job, spread the paint evenly onto the work surface without letting it run, drip, or lap onto other areas. Excess paint will run on the surface and can drip onto woodwork and floors. Stretching paint too far leaves lap marks and results in patchy coverage.

Start each section by "cutting in" with a brush on all edges, corners, and trim. Painting flat surfaces with brushes and rollers is a three-step process. First, apply the paint to the work surface, then distribute it evenly. Finally, smooth it out for a seamless finish.

How to Use a Paint Brush

Dip the brush, loading one-third of its bristle length. Tap the bristles against the side of the can. Dipping deeper overloads the brush. Dragging the brush against the lip of the can causes the bristles to wear.

Cut in the edges using the narrow edge of the brush, pressing just enough to flex the bristles. Keep an eye on the paint edge, and paint with long, slow strokes. Always paint from a dry area back into wet paint to avoid lap marks.

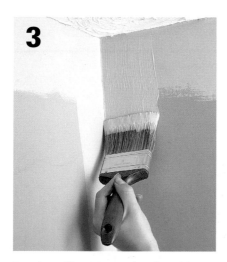

Brush wall corners using the wide edge of the brush. Paint open areas with a brush or roller before the brushed paint dries.

To paint large areas with a brush, apply the paint with 2 or 3 diagonal strokes. Hold the brush at a 45° angle to the work surface, pressing just enough to flex the bristles. Distribute the paint evenly with horizontal strokes.

Smooth the surface by drawing the brush vertically from the top to the bottom of the painted area. Use light strokes and lift the brush from the surface at the end of each stroke. This method is best for slow-drying alkyd enamels.

8. Roller Techniques

Paint surfaces in small sections, working from dry surfaces back into wet paint to avoid roller marks.

If a paint job takes more than a day, cover the roller tightly with plastic wrap or store it in a bucket of water overnight to prevent the paint from drying out.

Wet the roller cover with water (when painting with latex paint) or mineral spirits (when painting with alkyd enamel), to remove lint and prime the roller cover. Squeeze out excess liquid. Fill the paint tray reservoir. Dip the roller fully into the reservoir to load it with paint. Lift the roller from the paint reservoir, and roll it back and forth on the textured ramp to distribute the paint evenly onto the nap. The roller should be full, but not dripping, when lifted from the paint pan.

How to Paint With a Paint Roller

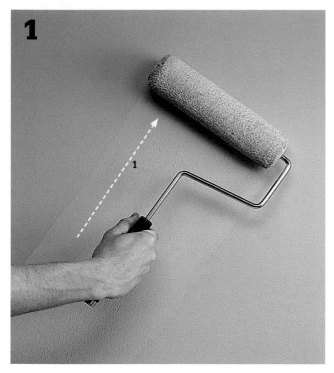

With the loaded roller, make a diagonal sweep (1) about 4' long on the surface. On walls, roll upward on the first stroke to avoid spilling paint. Use slow roller strokes to avoid splattering.

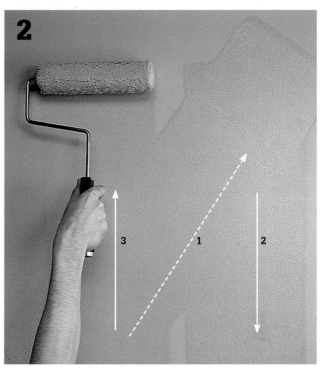

Draw the roller straight down (2) from top of the diagonal sweep. Shift the roller to the beginning of the diagonal and roll up (3) to complete the unloading of the roller.

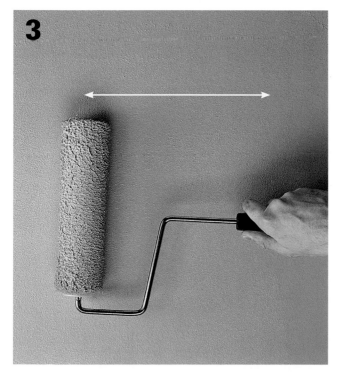

Distribute paint over the rest of the section with horizontal back-and-forth strokes.

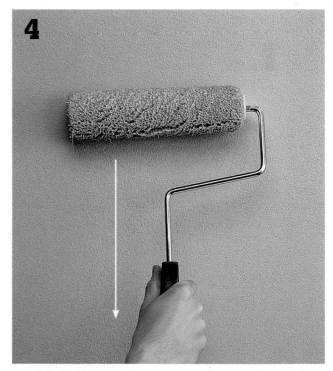

Smooth the area by lightly drawing the roller vertically from the top to the bottom of the painted area. Lift the roller and return it to the top of the area after each stroke.

9. Trim Techniques

When painting an entire room, paint the wood trim first, then paint the walls. Start by painting the inside portions of the trim, and work out toward the walls. On windows, for instance, first paint the edges close to the glass, then paint the surrounding face trim.

Doors should be painted quickly because of the large surface. To avoid lap marks, always paint from dry surfaces back into wet paint. On baseboards, cut in the top edge and work down to the flooring. Plastic floor guards or a wide broadknife can help shield carpet and wood flooring from paint drips.

Alkyds and latex enamels may require two coats. Always sand lightly between coats and wipe with a tack cloth so that the second coat bonds properly.

How to Paint a Window

1

To paint double-hung windows, remove them from their frames if possible. Newer, spring-mounted windows are released by pushing against the frame (see arrow).

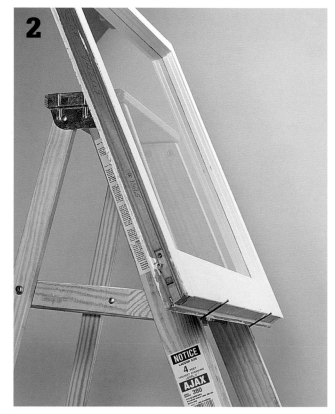

2

Drill holes and insert two 2" nails into the legs of a wooden step ladder. Mount the window easel-style for easy painting. Or, lay the window flat on a bench or sawhorses. Do not paint the sides or bottom of the window sashes.

3

Using a tapered sash brush, begin by painting the wood next to the glass. Use the narrow edge of the brush, and overlap the paint onto the glass to create a weatherseal.

4

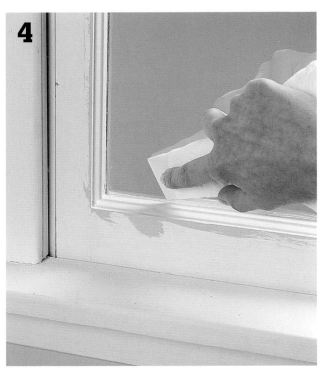

Remove excess paint from the glass with a putty knife wrapped in a clean cloth. Rewrap the knife often so that you always wipe with clean fabric. Overlap paint from the sash onto the glass by 1/16".

5

Case molding

Sash

Sill

Apron

Paint all flat portions of the sashes, then the case moldings, sill, and apron. Use slow brush strokes, and avoid getting paint between the sash and the frame.

6

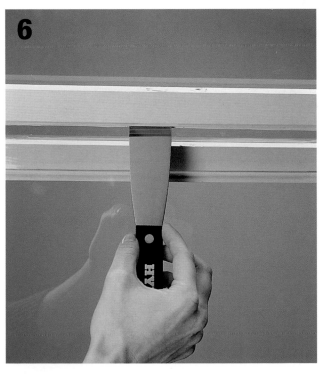

If you must paint windows in place, move the painted windows up and down several times during the drying period to keep them from sticking. Use a putty knife to avoid touching the painted surfaces.

How to Paint Doors

Remove the door by driving out the lower hinge pin with a screwdriver and hammer. Have a helper hold the door in place. Then, drive out the middle and upper hinge pins.

Place the door flat on sawhorses for painting. On paneled doors, paint in the following order, using a brush rather than a roller: 1) recessed panels, 2) horizontal rails, and 3) vertical stiles.

Let the painted door dry. If a second coat of paint is needed, sand the first coat lightly and wipe the door with tack cloth before repainting.

Seal the unpainted edges of the door with a clear wood sealer to prevent moisture from entering the wood. Water can cause wood to warp and swell.

Protect wall and floor surfaces with a wide wallboard knife or a plastic shielding tool.

Wipe all of the paint off of the wallboard knife or shielding tool each time it is moved.

Paint both sides of cabinet doors. This provides an even moisture seal and prevents warping.

Paint deep patterned surfaces with a stiff-bristled brush, like this stenciling brush. Use small circular strokes to penetrate recesses.

10. Ceiling & Wall Techniques

For a smooth finish on large wall and ceiling areas, paint in small sections. First use a paintbrush to cut in the edges, then immediately roll the section before moving on. If brushed edges dry before the area is rolled, lap marks will be visible on the finished wall. Working in natural light makes it easier to spot missed areas.

Choose high-quality paint and tools and work with a full brush or roller to avoid lap marks and to ensure full coverage. Roll slowly to minimize splattering.

Tips for Painting Ceilings & Walls ▶

Paint to a wet edge. Cut in the edges on small sections with a paintbrush, then immediately roll the section. (Using a corner roller makes it unnecessary to cut in inside corners.) With two painters, have one cut in with a brush while the other rolls the large areas.

Minimize brush marks. Slide the roller cover slightly off of the roller cage when rolling near wall corners or a ceiling line. Brushed areas dry to a different finish than rolled paint.

How to Paint Ceilings

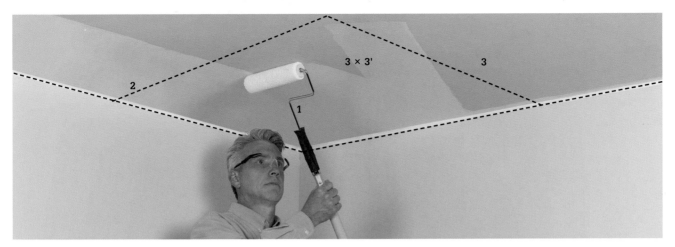

Paint ceilings with a roller handle extension. Use eye protection while painting overhead. Start at the corner farthest from the entry door. Paint the ceiling along the narrow end in 3 × 3' sections, cutting in the edges with a brush before rolling.

Apply the paint with a diagonal stroke. Distribute the paint evenly with back-and-forth strokes. For the final smoothing strokes, roll each section toward the wall containing the entry door, lifting the roller at the end of each sweep.

How to Paint Walls

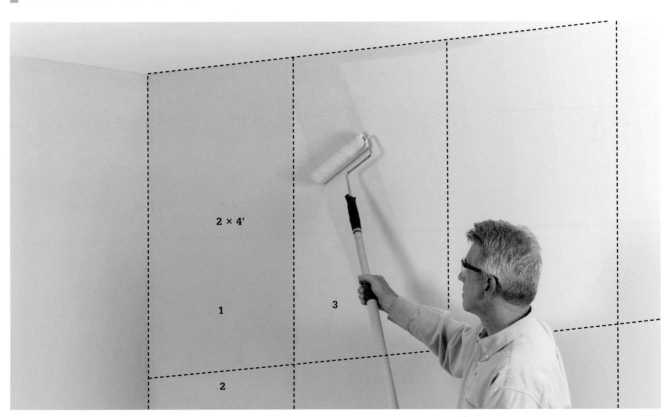

Paint walls in 2 × 4' sections. Start in an upper corner, cutting in the ceiling and wall corners with a brush, then rolling the section. Make the initial diagonal roller stroke from the bottom of the section upward, to avoid dripping paint. Distribute the paint evenly with horizontal strokes, then finish with downward sweeps of the roller. Next, cut in and roll the section directly underneath. Continue with adjacent areas, cutting in and rolling the top sections before the bottom sections. Roll all finish strokes toward the floor.

11. Texture Painting

Texture paints offer a decorating alternative to either flat paints or wallcoverings. The variety of possible effects you can achieve is limited only by your imagination. Texture paints are available in either premixed latex formulations or in dry powder form. Premixed latex texture paints are fine for producing light stipple patterns, but powder textures are a better choice for creating heavier adobe or stucco finishes. Powder textures are available in 25-lb. bags and must be mixed with water, using a paint mixer bit and power drill.

Practice texturing on cardboard until you get the pattern you want. Remember that the depth of the texture depends on the stiffness of the texture paint, the amount applied to the surface, and the type of tool used to create the texture.

Texturing Paint

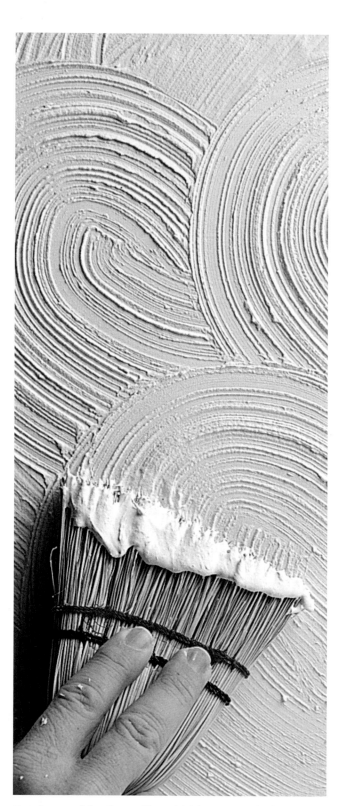

Use a long-nap roller to make this stipple texture effect. For different patterns, vary the pressure on the roller and amount of texture paint on the surface.

Create a swirl pattern with a whisk broom. Apply the texture paint with a roller, then use the broom to create the design.

Trowel texture material onto the surface, and pile the material in ridges to create an adobe pattern.

Dab, drag, or swirl a sponge through texture paint to create an endless variety of texture patterns. Or, let the first course dry, then sponge another color on top for a two-tone stucco effect.

Create a crowsfoot design by applying texture paint with a roller, brushing it out level, then randomly striking the surface with the flat side of the brush.

Press the flat side of a trowel into texture paint and pull it away to create a stomp design.

Trowel over a texture pattern when the paint has partially dried, to flatten peaks and achieve a brocade design. Clean the trowel between strokes with a wet brush or sponge.

12. Two-Color Meshing

Dozens of techniques can be used to produce interesting textured surfaces, but most require several steps. With this technique, you can create lovely color variations in only one step. It's quick and easy enough for any beginner.

This technique is designed to be used with satin-finish, standard latex paints—no glazes are necessary. In fact, glazes are not compatible with this technique.

When choosing paint, start by choosing your lightest color, and then find a second color that is three to five shades darker than the first. Colors that are three shades apart produce muted variations, while colors that are five shades apart produce more dramatic textures.

Tools & Materials ▸

Dual roller   Edging tool
Two-compartment   Masking tape
  paint tray   Two colors of satin-
1-inch brush   finish latex paint

How to Apply Meshed Color

1

Select two colors of satin-finish latex paint, one color three-to-five shades darker than the other. Stir the paint well, then pour each color into one compartment of a divided paint tray.

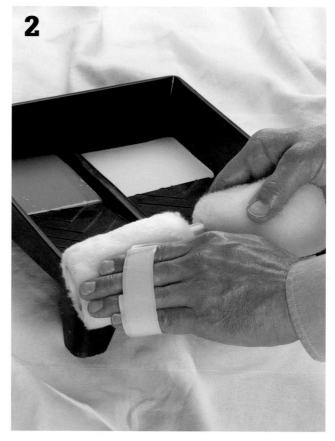

2

Remove any lint from the paint roller by patting it with the sticky side of masking tape. Change the tape when it loses its stickiness, and continue patting until no more lint comes off the roller. Dampen the roller with water and thoroughly wring it out.

3

Roll the two-color roller into the paint and run it up and down the textured portion of the tray several times. Make sure the roller is loaded well, but not so full that it will drip.

4

Make a diagonal sweep about two feet long, rolling slowly enough to avoid splatters. Make a second diagonal sweep in the opposite direction, then a third, sweep vertical.

5

Draw the roller in a back and forth motion until the colors are blended to your satisfaction.

6

At the edges and in corners, apply ample splotches of each paint color, using a 1" brush. Immediately pat the paint with the accessory pad to blend the colors to match the surrounding area.

13. Taped-off Designs

Tools & Materials ▶

Simple techniques using painter's masking tape can help you create stripes and geometric designs of all kinds. Select a professional-quality tape that prevents paint seepage and can be removed easily without damaging the base coat. For best results, apply the paint in light coats, but be careful not to thin the paint too much.

Alternating colors produce striking results; so does alternating between flat paint and a gloss finish. Whatever type of design you choose, measure the room and plan the pattern so it works out evenly around the room.

Carpenter's level
Pencil
Tape Measure
Small paint roller
Sponge applicator

Paintbrush or paint
  roller, for base coat
Latex or craft acrylic
  paints
Painter's masking tape

A laser level makes applying tape for the stripes practically foolproof. If you plan on doing a large project or several taped-off designs throughout your home, consider purchasing one.

How to Paint A Striped Design

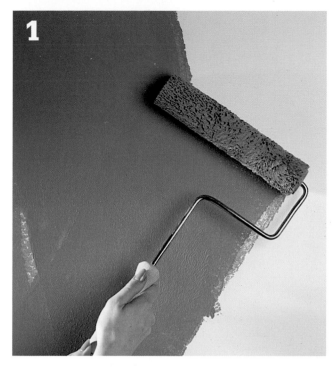

Apply a base coat in the desired color. Allow the paint to dry completely.

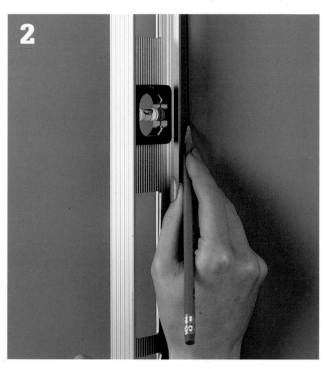

Mark light plumb lines for the first stripe, using a pencil and a carpenter's level. Apply painter's masking tape along the lines, and press the edges firmly to ensure a good bond.

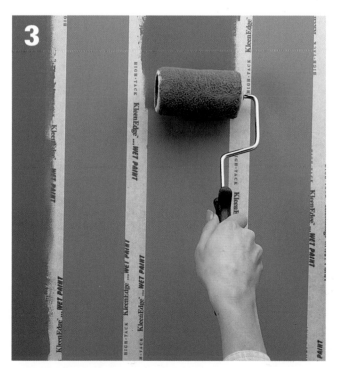

Measure from the first stripe, and draw parallel lines for the remaining stripes of the first color. Use the level to plumb each line. Apply the masking tape. Paint the stripes, using a paint-brush, small roller, or sponge applicator. Allow the paint to dry.

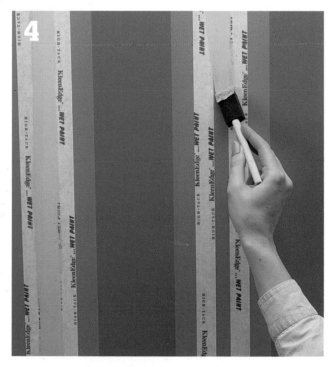

Remove the masking tape from the painted stripes. Repeat the process for any additional colors.

How to Apply an Alternating Matte and Gloss Finish

Fill all dents and holes, and sand away any bumps or ridges on the walls. (The gloss finish will magnify any surface flaws, so the walls must be perfectly flat and flawless.) Check the surface with a strong sidelight.

Tools & Materials ▸

Large paintbrush
1" paintbrush
Flat, square artist's
  brush
Pencil
Straightedge

Laser level or
  carpenter's level
Matte latex paint
High-gloss acrylic
  varnish

Variation ▸

If a flawless surface cannot be achieved on the walls, hang heavy-duty lining paper before starting the project.

Apply two coats of matte latex paint over the walls. Let the paint dry according to manufacturer's instructions.

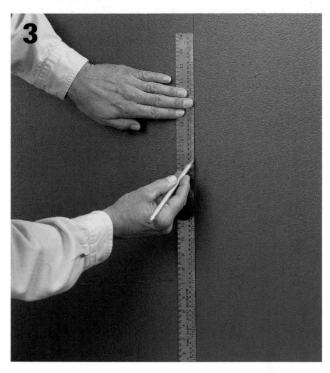

Measure walls and plan the design. Divide the height of the room until you find dimensions that will result in full squares at the baseboard and ceiling. Use a laser level or carpenter's level and a straightedge to draw the vertical and then the horizontal lines of the design.

Tape off the outline of every other square. Press the edges of the tape to ensure a good bond and seal the edges.

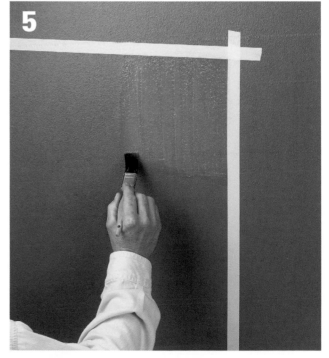

Apply a coat of high-gloss varnish within the taped-off squares. Allow the varnish to dry, and then apply a second coat. Remove the tape.

14. Sponge Painting

Sponge painting produces a soft, mottled effect and is one of the easiest techniques to master. The look of sponge painting is determined by the number of paint colors applied, the sequence in which they are applied, and the distance between the sponge impressions.

The sponge used is crucial. You can use a natural sea sponge, which will produce small, condensed marks, or sculpt a synthetic sponge to create a larger, more defined pattern.

Semigloss, satin, and flat latex paints all are appropriate for sponge painting. For a translucent finish, you can use a paint glaze consisting of paint, paint conditioner, and water (see Sponging Glaze below).

Before starting your project, select the sponge and paint colors, and practice on a piece of mat board or a scrap of drywall until you're satisfied with the effect.

Tools & Materials ▸

Paintbrushes and
   rollers for base
   coat
Roller tray
Large synthetic
   sponge
Latex paint for

base coat
Latex paint in two
   colors, one light and
   one dark
Latex paint conditioner
   (optional)

Sponging Glaze ▸

Mix together the following ingredients:
   1 part latex or craft acrylic paint
   1 part latex paint conditioner
   1 part water

How to Sponge Paint

Apply a coat of the base color, and let it dry completely.

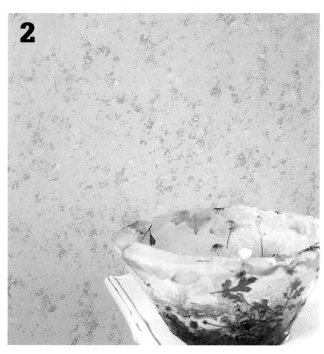

Tear out small chunks from the surface and around the edges of one side of the sponge. Make sure the entire surface is pitted with holes of various depths. Dampen the sponge and squeeze out as much of the water as possible.

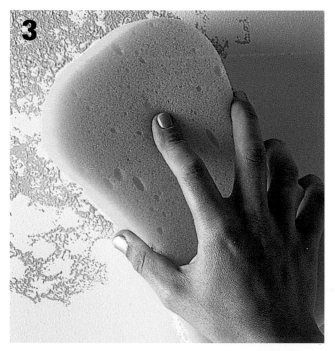

Pour some of the darker color into a roller tray, and press the pitted surface of the sponge into the paint. Pat the sponge onto a paper towel to remove the excess paint, and then use it to dab paint onto the wall. (Use a small chunk of the sponge to sponge paint into the corners.)

Working quickly, keep sponging until the surface is filled with sponged paint, but the base coat is still visible. (This layer will look fairly stark, but the next layer will soften it.) Let the paint dry. Wash out the paint tray and the sponge.

(continued next page)

5

Dampen the sponge again. Pour the lighter color into the paint tray, and press the sponge into it. Remove the excess paint on a paper towel.

6

Sponge the lighter color evenly over the wall. Cover the area, but don't completely cover the base coat or the first color. Use a small chunk of the sponge to apply the lighter color in the corners and at the edges of the wall. Stand back from the wall and evaluate the effect. Sponge more paint where necessary to even out the variations.

Sponging Tip ▶

For best results, try to keep a consistent amount of paint on the sponge.

How to Sponge Paint Stripes, Borders, or Panels

1

Apply sponge paint as described on pages 36 through 38, and let the paint dry. Tape off stripes (see page 33).

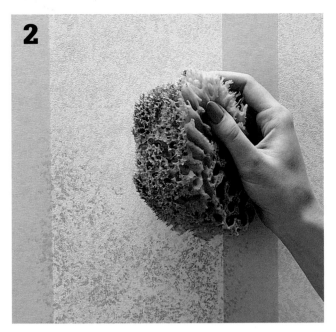

2

Apply an additional color to the unmasked areas. Blot or feather the paint, as desired. When the paint is dry, carefully remove the masking tape.

Sponging Variations ▶

To achieve a harmonious look, use related colors for sponge painting, such as two warm colors or two cool colors.

For a bolder and more unexpected look, sponge paint with a combination of warm and cool colors.

Cool colors, like green and blue, blend together for a tranquil effect.

Warm colors, like yellow and orange, blend together for an exciting effect.

Warm and cool colors, like yellow and blue, combine boldly, but sponge painting softens the effect.

15. Terra-Cotta Finish

Introduce depth, textures, and warmth to a room by giving the walls a terra-cotta finish. Although this finish has a sophisticated appearance, it's quite easy to create, even for a beginner. Unlike many other faux finishes, a terra-cotta finish does not require a preliminary base coat. Instead, you use a wool pad to apply and blend several colors of paint. The more you blend the paints, the more muted the finish becomes. Faux finish kits and wood pads are available at paint retailers and home centers.

The finish shown here was created with three shades of latex paint: deep brown, dark clay, and apricot. The overall hue of the finish depends on the colors you choose. For a rosier finish, select colors with a red base. Or, if you prefer an orange overtone, select colors with a yellow base. If you're not sure which colors to choose, your paint retailer can help you find the right combination.

Tools & Materials ▸

Divided paint tray
Paint stirrer sticks
Wool paint pad
Wool finishing tool

Brown, clay, and
    apricot latex paint
Paint glaze

How to Produce a Terra-Cotta Finish with a Wool Pad

Pour each shade of paint into a separate section of a divided paint tray. Add a quarter cup of paint glaze to each color, blending it into the paint with a stir stick. Wet your hand with water and run it over the wool pad to remove lint and loose fibers.

Dip the wool pad into the brown paint, and scrape the pad along the edge of the tray to remove excess paint. Working in 4' × 4' sections, apply the paint by pressing the pad to the wall in a random pattern. Cover about 80% of the wall surface in each section, leaving some bare spots visible.

Scrape the pad to remove as much of the brown paint from the pad as possible. You do not need to wash the pad before applying the next paint color.

(continued)

4

Dip the wool pad into the clay paint, and scrape off the excess. Using the same stamping technique you used to apply the brown paint, fill in the bare spots in the section with the clay paint. When you are finished, scrape the clay paint from the pad, as before.

5

Dip the wool pad into the apricot paint, and remove the excess. Using the random stamping technique, lightly press the wool pad onto the painted section. You will begin to see the paint blend. The more you apply the apricot paint, the more the paint will blend and the lighter the final design will be.

6

Once you've finished the section, use a finishing tool to apply paint in the corners and at the edges of the section. First, remove lint and loose fibers from the tool (see Step 1). Repeat Steps 2 through 5, applying the brown, clay, and apricot paints, blending until the design is complete. When the section is complete, move on to the next.

Tip ▶

Wool pads can be used to create a variety of finishes. Follow the same stamping technique used to create the terra-cotta finish, combining two or more colors. Or, apply a base coat and then use a glaze-removal technique to create a dragged finish.

Tone-on-Tone: Select two paints that are three or four colors apart on a monochromatic paint selection strip, one in a dark shade and one in a light shade. Apply the dark color first. Using the random stamping technique, cover nearly all of the 4' × 4' section. Then, apply the lighter color, stamping it in until the paints are blended to create the desired effect.

Contrasting Tones: Combine a contrasting color with two shades of the same color for a bold, eye-catching pattern. Apply the same-color shades first, starting with the darker shade, then the lighter. Apply the contrasting shade last, taking care not to blend it too much. If you overblend, the colors will become muddy and you'll lose the effect of the contrasting shade.

Metallic Accent: Create a striking design by using the wool pad to apply a metallic glaze over a tone-on-tone finish. Begin by painting a tone-on-tone finish. Use another clean wool pad to lightly tap on a metallic glaze with a quick stamping motion. If you stamp too much, you'll overblend the glaze and lose the effect.

Dragged Texture: This is a glaze removal technique. Apply a base coat of paint and let it dry. Make a glaze (see page 37) and roll a coat over a 4-foot-wide strip, from the ceiling to the floor. With a clean wool pad, start at the top of the wall and drag the pad down, moving it in a straight line. Wipe the pad on a lint-free cloth, and start again at the top of the wall. Repeat until the wall is completed.

16. Faux Panels

Trompe l'oeil effects "fool the eye" into seeing more than is there. In this case, a chair rail and some paint imitate wood paneling, creating depth and texture on plain walls.

The trickiest part of this project is deciding on the size of the "panels." The dimensions for every project will be slightly different because the panels have to be tailored to the size of the room and length of the walls. Measure the walls in question and calculate a size that produces complete panels on as many walls as possible.

For this technique to succeed, the walls need to be in very good condition before you begin. The wood-panel effect is created by dragging and lining, both of which need to be done on smooth, flat surfaces to ensure straight lines. Prepare the walls carefully.

Tools & Materials ▸

Large paintbrush
2" paintbrush
Dragging brush
Small fitch brush
Ruler
Carpenter's level or laser level
Pencil
Paint pail or bucket
Pale beige matte latex paint
Nut brown matte latex paint

How to Paint Faux Panels

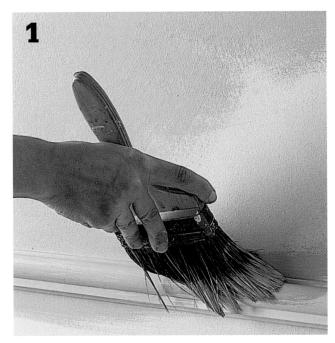

Apply two coats of pale beige paint to the entire project area, including the chair rail. (If the room does not have a chair rail, install one 30 to 36" above the floor.)

Measure and draw panels in proportion to the length of the wall and height of the chair rail. Use a carpenter's level or a laser level to make sure the lines are perfectly straight.

Mask off the horizontal "boards" above and below the central square of each panel.

(continued)

Mix equal parts of nut brown paint and water in a pail or bucket. Dip a clean 2" paintbrush into the diluted paint and pat it on clean paper towels to remove the excess. Brush the paint vertically onto one "board" at a time.

While the paint is still wet, hold a dragging brush at the top of the "board." Place your fingers near the tip of the bristles to control them, and pull the brush down through the wet paint. Keep the lines as straight as possible. Continue until you've painted and dragged all the vertical "boards" on the wall. Paint and drag the central square of each panel on the wall. Remove the masking tape and allow the paint to dry.

Mask off the vertical panels in preparation for painting the horizontal "boards." Using the same nut-brown wash and the same dragging technique, paint and drag the horizontal parts of the panels. Drag the brush through the wet paint in the same direction on each "board" on the wall. Remove the masking tape and let the paint dry.

7

Paint the wash over the chair rail, using long, sweeping strokes. The goal is to create the same type of "grain" on the chair rail as on the "panels."

8

Use a small brush and the nut brown wash to create shadows at the edges of the panels. Paint a narrow band around the edges of the central square to create the illusion that the areas around the square are raised.

9

If a drag isn't straight enough, run over the paint again while it is still wet. It can be helpful to hang a plumb bob or shoot a laser line to act as a guide while you drag.

17. Blended Color Bands

This blending technique creates the illusion that the colors are fading into one another, an unusual and striking effect that's easy to produce and delightful in many settings.

The success of this technique depends heavily upon good color selection. Choose two paint colors that sit next to each other on the color wheel. You'll create the third color by mixing together equal amounts of each. The resulting midtone will smooth the transition between the top and bottom bands and enhance the illusion.

The paint has to be wet in order to blend the bands properly, so it's best to work on short sections at a time. If the paint gets too dry to blend the way you want, add fresh paint to each band, and blend it again.

Tools & Materials ▶

Carpenter's level or	Power drill and
laser level	paint-mixing bit
Tape measure	Three paint pails
Straightedge	Two colors of matte
Pencil	latex paint
Five 3" paintbrushes	Wallpaper paste

How to Create Blended Color Bands

1

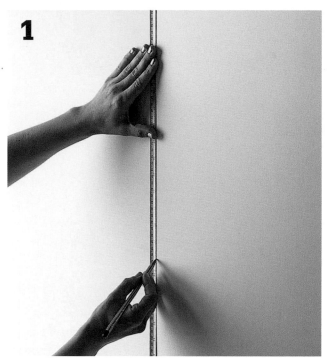

Measure the wall and divide it into three equal sections. Using a laser or carpenter's level, draw horizontal lines to act as guidelines for the bands of paint.

2

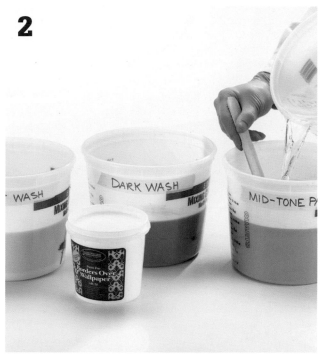

Pour equal amounts of each color into a pail and use a drill and paint-mixing bit to blend it thoroughly. In a second pail, mix equal amounts of the darkest paint and wallpaper paste. In a third, mix equal amounts of the lightest paint and wallpaper paste. Label the pails.

3

Paint a 2'- to 3' section of the darkest color at the bottom of the wall, spreading the paint roughly up to the first guideline.

(continued)

4

Apply a coat of the blended mid-tone (created in Step 2) to a 2' to 3' section of the middle band. Leave an inch or so between this band and the first one.

5

Apply a thick coat of the dark wash to the gap between the first and second bands. Dampen a clean paintbrush and run it along the line between the bands, blending the wash up and down into each band until the lines have disappeared into a subtle transition between colors.

6

Apply the lightest color to the top band, leaving a gap between it and the middle band. Apply a thick coat of the light wash between the bands, and then use a clean, damp paintbrush to blend the colors up and down as before.

7

Continue painting one section of the wall at a time, running over at the corners. Use the finished corner as a placement guide for the newly painted one, blending the edges to make sure the color shifts are consistent. Slight variations are inevitable, but try to keep the blends as consistent as possible.

18. Color Wash Finishes

Color washing is an easy finish that gives walls a translucent, water-colored look. It adds visual texture to flat surfaces and can emphasize textured surfaces. There are two basic methods of color washing, each with its own glaze mixture and appearance.

The sponge method of color washing calls for a highly diluted glaze that is applied over a base coat of low-luster latex enamel, using a natural sea sponge. The result is a subtle texture with a soft blending of colors. The other method is color washing with a paintbrush, using a heavier glaze that holds more color than the sponge glaze. This finish retains the fine lines of the brush strokes to create a more dramatic play of tones. As the glaze begins to dry, it can be softened further by brushing the surface with a dry, natural-bristle paintbrush.

The color wash glaze can be either lighter or darker than the base coat. For best results, use two colors that are closely related, or consider using a neutral color, like beige or white, for either the base coat or the glaze. Because the glaze is messy to work with, cover the floor and furniture with drop cloths, and apply painter's tape along the ceiling and moldings.

Tools & Materials ▶

Paint roller
Flat latex paint, for glaze
Latex paint conditioner, for sponge glaze
Pail
Rubber gloves
Painter's masking tape

Natural sea sponge or two 3" to 4" natural-bristle paintbrushes
Waterproof drop cloths
Low-luster latex enamel paint, for base coat

How to Color Wash with a Sponge

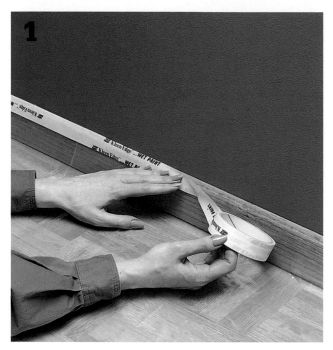

Sponge Color Wash Glaze ▸

Mix together the following ingredients:

- 1 part latex or acrylic paint
- 8 parts water

Brush Color Wash Glaze ▸

Mix together the following ingredients:

- 1 part flat latex paint
- 1 part latex paint conditioner
- 2 parts water

Mask off the surrounding area, using painter's masking tape, and cover the floor with waterproof drop cloths. Apply a base coat of low-luster latex enamel paint, using a paint roller. Allow the paint to dry.

Immerse the sponge into the color-washing solution. Squeeze out excess liquid, but leave the sponge very wet.

Beginning in a low corner, wipe the color wash solution onto the wall in short, curving strokes. Overlap and change the direction of the strokes, quickly covering a 3' × 3' section of wall.

Repeat Steps 2 and 3, moving upward and outward until the entire wall has been color washed. Allow the paint to dry. Apply a second coat if additional color is desired.

How to Color Wash with a Brush

1

Apply a base coat of low-luster latex enamel, using a paint roller. Allow the paint to dry. Mix the color-washing glaze in a pail. Dip a paintbrush into the glaze, and remove excess glaze by scraping the brush against the rim of the pail. Apply the glaze to the wall in a cross-hatching manner, beginning in one corner. The more you brush, the softer the appearance will be.

2

Brush over the surface if desired, using a dry natural-bristle paintbrush, to soften the look. Wipe excess glaze from the brush as necessary.

Color Wash Variations ▶

Select colors for the base coat and the glaze that are closely related, or use at least one neutral color.

A darker glaze over a lighter base coat gives a mottled effect. A lighter glaze over a darker base coat gives a chalky or watercolored effect.

A medium turquoise top coat was applied over a lighter base coat of white.

A coral base coat was covered with a white top coat.

19. Stamped Mosaic

Mosaic tile is a classic choice for walls, but tile can be expensive and time-consuming to install. A painted mosaic is inexpensive and easy to do, and can be changed just as easily as it can be created.

The effect of a tile mosaic is too dramatic to use it in large spaces. Typically, it's best to choose a small area or the space below a chair rail for this finish. With its irregular coloration and varied pattern, a painted mosaic can cover many flaws, so the preparation steps for this project don't have to be quite as elaborate as for many other paint projects.

Tools & Materials ▸

Craft knife
Large paintbrush
Roller and roller tray
Three 1" brushes
Small artist's brush
Repositionable
    spray glue
Ruler
High-density
    foam rubber
Low-tack masking tape
Three colors of latex
    paint

Apply two coats of paint to the entire wall, including the chair rail. Let the second coat dry completely, and then mask off the edges of the chair rail and baseboard.

How to Create a Stamped Mosaic

Place some of each paint color into the well of a clean roller tray. Using three clean paintbrushes, dab a generous amount of each color of paint onto the flat surface of the roller tray. It's fine for the colors to blend a little in a few places, but don't deliberately mix them.

To make a paper template for the stamp, draw a series of tiles divided by quarter-inch grout lines. Round the corners of the squares to resemble tile. Spray the back of the paper with repositionable spray glue and press the pattern onto the high-density foam. Cut around each tile, using a craft knife, and remove the excess pieces. (Try to consistently cut about halfway into the foam.) When the stamp is complete, press it into the paint until it's well coated but not dripping with paint.

Start in the top, left-hand corner of the area to be decorated. Press the stamp squarely against the wall, being careful not to let it slip. After a moment, peel the stamp away from the wall, pulling it back from one side. Recoat the stamp and position it next to the previous print. Leave a quarter-inch gap to create a grout line. Continue stamping until the project is complete.

When stamping below a previous row, align the pattern lines before pressing the stamp to the wall. When adding more paint to the tray, keep the colors separate enough to create the mottled effect you're working toward. If the tiles bleed together, reestablish the base color with a small artist's brush (inset).

20. Stenciled Designs

Stenciled motifs can be used to highlight an area or feature of a room or to mimic architectural details such as chair rails or crown molding.

Before beginning a project, carefully plan the placement of the design. Measure the walls and create an arrangement that doesn't produce any partial repeats. When you've come up with a plan, stencil the design on paper and tape it to the wall to make sure it works as planned. Start in the most prominent area, and work outward. If it's necessary to avoid interruptions, such as windows, doors, or heating vents, you can slightly alter the spacing between repeats to accommodate them.

Most precut stencils have a separate plate for each color and are numbered according to the sequence of use. A single plate sometimes is used for several colors if the spaces between the design areas are large enough to be covered with masking tape. When using stencils of this type, apply the largest part of the design first. When stenciling borders, it's generally best to apply all the repeats of the first color before applying the second color.

You can make custom stencils by tracing designs onto transparent Mylar sheets and cutting them out. To coordinate stencils with home furnishing such as wallpaper, fabric, or artwork, use a photocopy machine to enlarge or reduce the patterns to the desired size, and then adapt a design from them.

For painting hard surfaces, such as walls and woodwork, use craft acrylic paint or oil-based stencil paint in liquid or solid form. After stenciling over finished wood, apply a coat of clear finish or sealer to the entire surface.

How to Make a Custom Stencil

Tools & Materials ▶

Paper
Colored pencils
Transparent Mylar sheets
Masking tape
Fine-point permanent-ink
    marking pen
Cutting surface, such as
    a self-healing cutting
    board or cardboard
Mat knife
Metal ruler

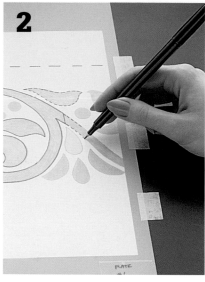

Draw or trace the design onto a sheet of paper. Repeat the design, if necessary, so it is 13" to 18" long, making sure the spacing between repeats is consistent. Color the design, using colored pencils. Mark placement lines to help you position the stencil on the wall.

Position a Mylar sheet over the design so the edges of the sheet extend beyond the top and bottom of the design by at least 1". Secure the sheet with masking tape. Trace the areas that will be stenciled in the first color, using a marking pen. Transfer the placement lines.

Trace the design areas for each additional color onto a separate Mylar sheet. To help you align the stencil, outline the areas for previous colors with dotted lines. Layer all of the Mylar sheets, and check for accuracy. Using a mat knife and straightedge, trim the outer edges of the stencil plates, leaving a 1" to 3" border around the design.

Separate the Mylar sheets. Cut out the traced areas on each sheet, using a mat knife. Cut the smallest shapes first, then cut the larger ones. Pull the knife toward you as you cut, turning the Mylar sheet, rather than the knife, to change the cutting direction.

How to Stencil on Hard Surfaces

1

2

Tools & Materials ▶

Carpenter's level
  and pencil
Stencil brushes
Artist's brush
Precut or custom stencil
Masking tape
Spray adhesive, optional
Craft acrylic paints, or
  liquid or solid oil-based
  stencil paints
Clear wood finish and
  paintbrush if stenciling
  on wood
Disposable plates
Paper towels

Mark the placement for the stencil on the surface with masking tape. Or, draw a light reference line, using a carpenter's level and a pencil. Position the stencil plate for the first color, aligning the placement line with the tape or pencil line. Secure the stencil in place, using masking tape or spray adhesive.

Place 1 to 2 tsp. of acrylic or oil-based paint on a disposable plate. Dip the tip of a stencil brush into the paint. Blot the brush onto a folded paper towel, using a circular motion, until the bristles are almost dry.

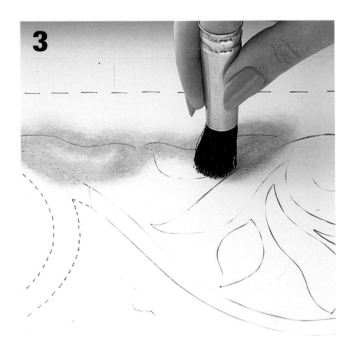

3

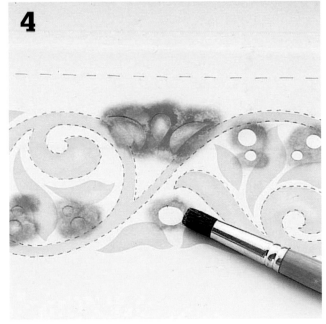

4

Hold the brush perpendicular to the surface. Apply the paint within the cut areas of the stencil, using a circular motion. Stencil all of the cut areas of the first stencil plate, and allow the paint to dry. Remove the stencil.

Secure the second plate to the surface, matching the design. Apply the second paint color in all of the cut areas. Repeat the process for any remaining stencils and colors unitl the design is completed. After all of the paints are completely dry, touch up any glitches or smudges on the surface, using background paint and an artist's brush.

Stenciling Variations ▸

To stencil with solid paint, or crayon paint, remove the protective coating from the crayon tip, using a paper towel. Rub a 1½" circle of paint onto a blank area of the stencil. Load a stencil brush by lightly rubbing the brush over the paint in a circular motion, first in one direction, then in the other direction.

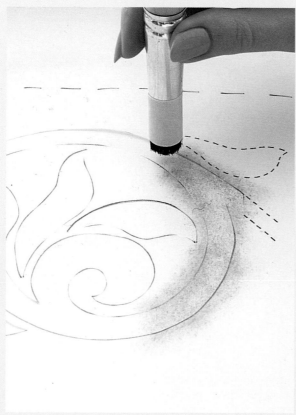

While the circular method of stenciling results in a blended finish, the stippling method produces a deeper, textured appearance. To stipple, wrap masking tape around the bristles of a stenciling brush, ¼" from the ends. Hold the brush perpendicular to the surface, and apply the paint using a dabbing motion. This method is also used to stencil fabric.

Techniques for Shaded Designs

1

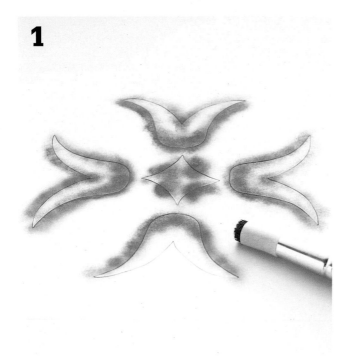

Apply paint within the cut areas of the stencil, leaving the centers lighter than the edges. For an aged, fade-away effect, use a heavier touch at the base of the motif and a lighter touch at the top.

2

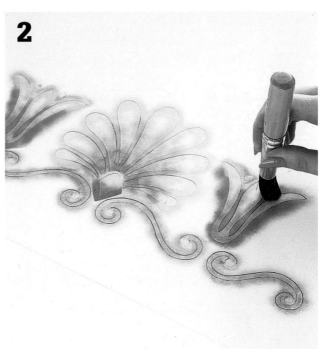

Apply a complementary or darker color of paint, shading the outer edges of the cut areas.

3

Apply paint to the outer edges of the cut areas and allow it to dry. Hold a piece of Mylar in place to cover a portion of the area, and apply paint next to the edge of the Mylar. For example, cover one-half of a leaf to stencil the veins.

Cleaning Stencil Brushes ▸

Clean stencil brushes used to apply acrylic paints by applying a small amount of dishwashing detergent to the brush. Rub the bristles in the palm of your hand in a circular motion until all of the paint is removed. Rinse with water and allow the bristles to dry. To remove oil-based paint, first clean the brush with mineral spirits and dry it on paper towels. Then, wash the brush with detergent and rinse with water.

21. Scumbled Wall Designs

Scumbling is a simple painting technique you can use to create textural geometric patterns that mimic the look of expensive wallcovering. With this technique, a large stencil brush is used to dry-brush paint onto the wall in swirling motions over a base coat. Because very little paint is required for dry-brushing, small jars of acrylic craft paints can be used. Choose two or three related decorator colors. Or, for a look that is classic and rich, use gold and silver metallic paints.

You can customize the geometric design, covering an entire wall, as shown in the diamond design on the opposite page. Or plan a chair rail in a block pattern, a ceiling border made of triangular shapes, or a striped wainscoting. Use painter's masking tape to mask off the designs.

Measure each wall, and sketch the geometric design on graph paper to help you determine the scale and placement of the design. Before painting the walls, experiment with the painting technique, making test samples on sheets of cardboard.

To prepare the surface, clean the walls, removing any dirt or grease, and rinse them with clear water. If the walls are unfinished, apply a primer and allow it to dry thoroughly before applying the masking tape.

Tools & Materials ▸

Ruler
Pencil
Paint roller
Carpenter's level
Straightedge
Putty knife
Stencil brush, 1" in
   diameter
Graph paper

Painter's masking
   tape
Latex paint, for base
   coat
Latex or craft
   acrylic paints, for
   scumbling
Disposable plates
Paper towels

How to Paint a Taped-off Scumbled Design

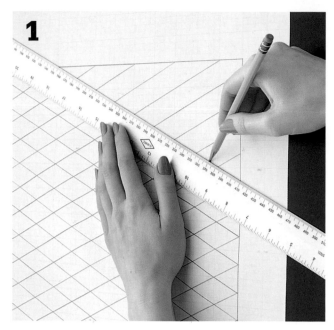

Measure the wall, and plan the design to scale on graph paper. Apply a base coat of paint, using a paint roller.

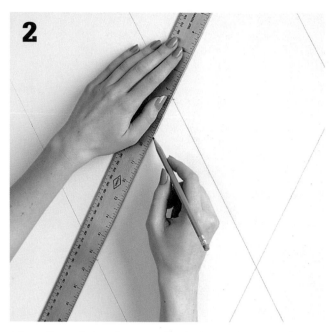

Allow the paint to dry. Draw the design on the wall with pencil, using a straightedge as a guide.

Mark the sections that will be masked off. Apply painter's masking tape to the marked sections, using a putty knife to trim the tape diagonally at the corners. Press along all edges of the tape, using a plastic credit card or your fingernail to create a tight seal.

Pour a small amount of each paint color onto a disposable plate. Dip the tip of the stencil brush into the first color. Using a circular motion, blot the brush onto a paper towel until the bristles are almost dry.

5

Brush the paint onto the wall with vigorous, wide, circular motions. Work in a small area at a time, and change the direction of the circular motions frequently. Overlap the paint onto the masking tape. Build up the color to the desired intensity, but allow the base coat to show through. Use all of the paint on bristles before applying more.

6

Dip the brush into the second color, and blot the brush. Apply the paint randomly over the same area, building up the color to varying intensities throughout the area. Repeat with a third color, if desired.

7

Repeat the technique to complete the entire wall, working in one small area at a time and blending areas together. Remove the masking tape when the paint is dry.

22. Strié & Combed Finishes

Strié and combed finishes are created by similar techniques in which a tool is dragged over wet glaze to reveal a base coat of a different color. The result is a textured, linear pattern, which can run in vertical lines, curves, swirls, zig-zags, or a weave pattern resembling fabric. Both finishes start with a base coat of low-luster latex enamel, followed by a latex or acrylic glaze mixture. The differences between these finishes are the result of the tools used to create the pattern.

The strié effect is created using a dry, natural-bristle brush, resulting in fine, irregular streaks and an interesting blend of color variations. A combed finish can be made with a variety of specialty tools, offering a range of patterns and designs. An additional option for the combed finish is to use a thickened glaze, which gives an opaque look and more distinct lines and texture.

Since the glaze must be wet for brushing or combing, timing is important with both techniques. For large surfaces, it is helpful to work with an assistant. After one person has applied the glaze, the other person brushes or combs through the glaze before it dries. If you are working alone, limit yourself to smaller sections. For best results, practice the technique and experiment with different glaze thicknesses by testing the finish on mat board before painting the wall.

Tools & Materials ▸

Paint roller or
  natural-bristle
  paintbrush
Wide natural-bristle
  brush
Soft natural-bristle
  paintbrush
Combing tool
Low-luster latex
enamel, for
  base coat
Latex paint in
  desired sheen and
  color, for glaze
Latex paint
  conditioner, such
  as loetrol
Rags

Basic Glaze ▸

Mix together the following ingredients:

- 1 part latex or craft acrylic paint
- 1 part latex paint conditioner
- 1 part water

Thickened Glaze ▸

Mix together the following ingredients:

- 2 parts latex or craft acrylic paint
- 1 part acrylic paint thickener
- (may be used with latex paints

How to Apply a Strié Paint Finish

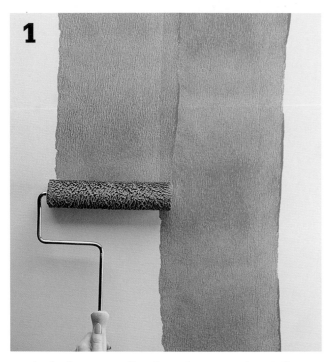

Apply the base coat of low-luster latex enamel, and allow 1the paint to dry. Mix the glaze (page 67). Apply the glaze over the base coat in a vertical section about 18" wide, using a paint roller or natural-bristle paintbrush.

Drag a dry, wide natural-bristle brush through the wet glaze, immediately after the glaze is applied; work from top to the bottom in continuous brush strokes. To keep the brush rigid, hold the bristles against the surface with the handle tilted slightly toward you. Repeat until the desired effect is achieved.

Wipe the paintbrush occasionally on a clean, dry rag to remove excess glaze and ensure a uniform strié look. Or, rinse the brush in clear water, and wipe it dry.

For softer lines, brush the surface lightly after the glaze has dried for about 5 minutes. Use a soft natural-bristle brush, keeping the brush stokes in the same direction as the streaks.

Techniques for Applying a Combed Finish ▸

Tools for combing include the Wagner Stipple and Drag pad (with edging tool), metal and rubber combs, and a notched rubber squeegee. You can make your own combing tools by notching an artist's eraser or cutting V grooves into a piece of mat board.

Create a unique check pattern, using a rubber comb. After each pass, wipe off the tool with a dry rag to prevent the glaze from building up and smearing the comb lines.

A Wagner Stipple and Drag pad can make a variety of combing designs. For a denim look, drag the pad through the glaze vertically, then horizontally

Use a rubber squeegee for swirls, scallops, and wavy lines. Wipe off excess glaze frequently to ensure clean lines.

23. Faux Moiré Finish

The watermarked look of silk moiré fabric can be created using a rocker tool designed for wood graining. A paint glaze is applied over a base coat of paint, and the graining tool is pulled and rocked through the glaze to create impressions. Then, a dry paintbrush is pulled across the markings to mimic the crosswise grain of moiré. This dramatic tone-on-tone finish is recommended for small areas, such as the space below a chair rail or within frame moldings.

The bright sheen that is characteristic of moiré fabric is simulated by using a darker shade of low-luster latex enamel for the base coat and a lighter shade for the top coat glaze. You can use the same paint for both coats by lightening the top coat with white paint.

The glaze used for faux moiré contains more paint than most glazes, making it thicker and more opaque. Apply the glaze to a small area at a time so that you will have enough time to finish the graining before the glaze dries. If you are finishing the wall area below a chair rail or border, work from the chair rail down to the baseboard in 12"-wide sections.

Tools & Materials ▸

- Wood-graining rocker tool
- Paint roller or paintbrush, for applying base coat and glaze
- Natural-bristle paintbrush, 2" to 3" wide, for dry brushing
- Low-luster latex enamel paint in darker shade, for base coat
- Low-luster enamel paint in lighter shade, or white paint to lighten base color, for glaze
- Latex paint conditioner
- Rags

How to Apply a Faux Moiré Finish

Faux Moiré Glaze ▸

Mix together the following ingredients:

2 parts semigloss latex enamel paint
1 part latex paint conditioner
1 part water

Apply the base coat of low-luster latex enamel, using a paint roller or paintbrush. Allow the paint to dry.

Mix the glaze for the top coat. Apply an even coat of glaze over the base, rolling or brushing vertically. Work in small areas to ensure the paint remains wet as you work it.

3

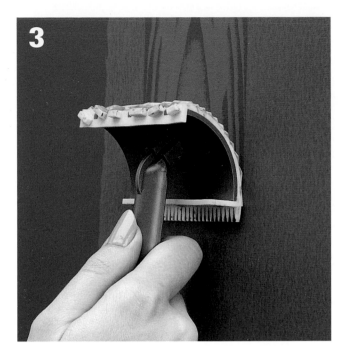

Slide the graining tool vertically through the wet glaze, occasionally rocking it slowly back and forth, to create the watermarked effect. Start at one corner, working in one continuous motion as you slide and rock the tool from one end to another. The simultaneous rocking and sliding motions create elongated oval markings.

4

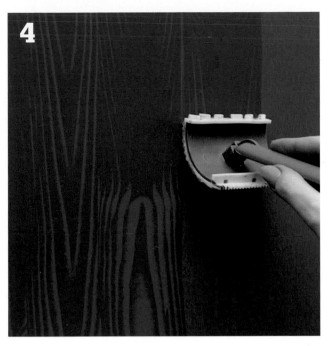

Repeat Step 3 for subsequent rows. Stagger the oval markings so that they appear randomly placed, and work quickly before glaze dries. Wipe the excess glaze from the tool as necessary, using a dry rag.

5

When the glaze has partially dried, pull a dry natural-bristle paintbrush horizontally across the surface; this mimics the crosswise grain of the moiré fabric. Wipe excess glaze from the brush as necessary. Allow the paint to dry.

24. Rag-rolled Designs

Rag rolling is a painting technique that gives a rich, textural look with an all-over mottled effect. It works well for walls and other flat surfaces, such as dresser tops and drawers, shelves, bookends, and doors. The rag-rolling glaze on page 76 can be used in either of the two techniques for rag rolling: ragging-on and ragging-off.

In ragging-on, a rag is saturated in the prepared paint glaze, wrung out, rolled up, then rolled across a surface that has been base-coated with low-luster latex enamel paint. For a bold pattern, rag-on a single application of glaze over the base coat. Or, for a more subtle, blended look, rag-on two or more applications of glaze.

In ragging-off, a coat of paint glaze is applied over the base coat with a paintbrush or paint roller. A rolled-up rag is then rolled over the surface to remove some of the wet glaze, revealing the base coat. This process may be repeated for more blending, but the work must be done quickly, before the glaze dries.

If you are using the ragging-off method on large surfaces, such as walls, it is helpful to have an assistant. After one person applies the glaze, the second person can rag-off the area before the glaze dries. While it is not necessary to complete the entire room in one session, it is important that you complete an entire wall.

With either method, test the technique and the colors that you intend to use on a large piece of cardboard, such as mat board, before you start the project. Generally, a lighter color is used for the base coat, with a darker color for the glaze.

Feel free to experiment with the technique as you test it, perhaps rag rolling two different glaze colors over the base coat. Or, try taping off an area, such as a border strip, and rag rolling a second or third color within the taped area.

Because the glaze can be messy to work with, apply a wide painter's tape around the area to be painted and use drop cloths to protect the surrounding surfaces. Wear old clothes and rubber gloves, and keep an old towel nearby to wipe your hands after you wring out the rags.

How to Apply a Rag-rolled Finish Using the Ragging-on Method

Rag-Rolling Glaze ▸

Mix together the following ingredients:

- 1 part latex or craft acrylic paint
- 1 part latex paint conditioner
- 1 part water

Tools & Materials ▸

Paintbrush or paint roller
Paint pail
Paint tray
Painter's masking tape
Low-luster latex enamel paint, for base coat

Latex or craft acrylic paint, for glaze
Latex paint conditioner
Rubber gloves
Lint-free rags, about 24" x 24"
Towel

Apply a base coat of low-luster latex enamel, using a paintbrush or paint roller. Allow the paint to dry. Mix the glaze in a pail. Dip a lint-free rag into the glaze, saturating the entire rag, then wring it out well. Wipe excess glaze from your hands with an old towel.

Roll up the rag irregularly, then fold it to a length equal to the width of both hands.

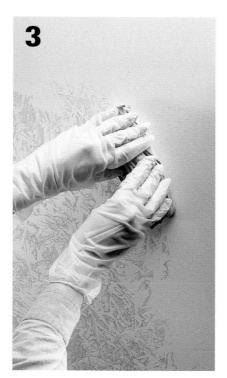

Roll the rag over the surface, working upward at varying angles. Rewet the rag whenever necessary, and wring it out.

Repeat the application, if more coverage is desired.

How to Apply a Rag-rolled Finish Using the Ragging-off Method

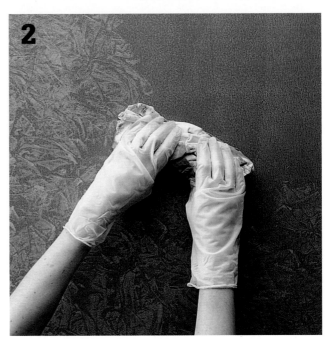

Apply base coat of low-luster latex enamel, using a paintbrush or paint roller. Allow the paint to dry. Mix the glaze (page opposite), and pour it into a paint tray. Apply the glaze over the base coat, using paint roller or paint pad.

Roll up a lint-free rag irregularly, then fold it to a length equal to the width of both hands. Roll the rag through the wet glaze, working upward at varying angles.

Techniques for Applying a Combed Finish ▸

As shown in the examples below, the color of the base coat is not affected when the ragging-on method is used.

With the ragging-off method, the color of the base coat is changed, because the glaze is applied over the entire surface.

Here, the ragging-on method was used to apply an aqua glaze over a white base coat. The white base coat remained unchanged.

The ragging-off method was used here to remove some of the aqua glaze from a white base coat. Because the base was covered with the glaze, the lighter areas appear as light aqua, rather than white.

Both ragging-on and ragging-off methods were used here. First, a taupe glaze was ragged-on over a white base coat, then a rust glaze was ragged-off, changing the white base coat to a lighter shade of rust.

25. Faux Serpentine Finish

Serpentine is the general name given to a variety of green marbles that contain deposits of the mineral serpentine. The different types vary in visual texture and color tone, often with traces of black and white. Some serpentines may be characterized by a network of fine veining, while others contain little or no veining. As with other marbles, the serpentines have been used for various architectural applications, including floors, walls, and pillars.

Because genuine marble is often cut into workable pieces for installation, a faux serpentine finish applied to a large surface is more realistic if it is applied in sections with narrow grout lines. By masking off alternate sections, the finish can be applied to half the project, following Steps 1 to 8. When the first sections have been allowed to dry completely, they can be masked off, and the finish can be applied to the remaining sections. A high-gloss finish is then applied to the entire surface, giving the faux finish the lustrous appearance of genuine marble.

Tools & Materials ▶

- Low-napped paint roller, for base coat on a large surface
- Sponge applicator or paintbrush
- Stippler
- Spray bottle
- Turkey feather, for veining
- Medium green low-luster latex enamel paint, for base
- coat
- Craft acrylic paints in green (darker than base coat), black, and white
- Water-based clear urethane
- Newspaper
- Cheesecloth
- High-gloss clear finish or high-gloss aerosol clear acrylic sealer

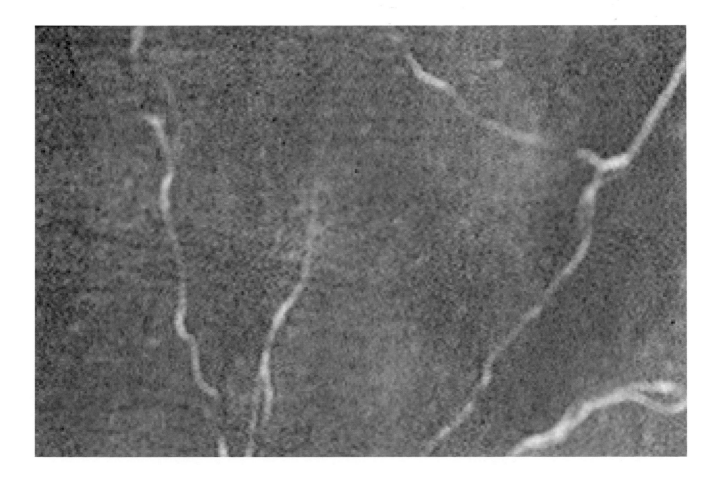

How to Apply a Rag-rolled Finish Using the Ragging-on Method

Faux Serpentine Gloss Glaze ▸

Mix together the following ingredients for each gloss glaze:

- 1 part clear urethane
- 1 part paint, in desired shade
- 1 part water

Apply a base coat of medium green low-luster latex enamel to the surface, using an applicator suitable to the surface size. Apply black, green, and white gloss glazes separately in random, broad, diagonal strokes, using a sponge applicator or paintbrush. Cover most of the surface, allowing small patches of the base coat to show through.

Stipple the glazes in adjoining areas to blend them slightly, bouncing a stippler rapidly over the surface.

Fold a sheet of newspaper to several layers and lay it flat over an area of the surface, in the same diagonal direction as the original paint strokes. Press the newspaper into the glaze, then lift it off, removing some of glaze.

Repeat Step 3 over the entire surface, using the same newspaper. Occasionally turn the paper in opposite directions. Add glazes as desired to develop the color, and soften areas of high contrast by dabbing with wadded cheesecloth. Mist the surface with water if necessary, to keep the glazes workable.

Brush black glaze onto a piece of newspaper and touch it to the surface diagonally in scattered areas, adding drama and depth. Soften with cheesecloth, if necessary. Repeat the process using a white glaze in small, light areas.

Dilute a mixture of white and green glazes with water to the consistency of light cream. Run the edge and tip of the feather through the diluted glaze. Place the tip of the feather onto the surface in the desired placement for a vein. Lightly drag the feather diagonally over the surface, fidgeting and turning it slightly, and varying the pressure, to create an irregular, jagged vein. Begin and end veins off the edge of the surface.

Repeat step 6 as desired to build a veining pattern. Connect adjacent vein lines occasionally to create narrow, oblong, irregular shapes. Dab veins lightly with wadded cheesecloth to soften, if necessary. Allow the surface to dry.

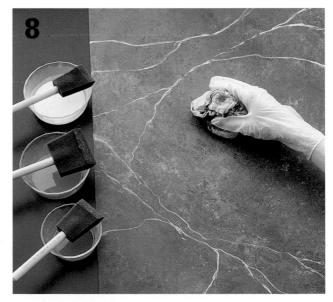

Dilute the glazes to the consistency of ink, and apply each randomly to the surface. Dab with wadded cheesecloth to soften the colors. Allow the glazes to dry. Apply several thin coats of high-gloss clear finish or high-gloss aerosol clear acrylic sealer, allowing the surface to dry between coats.

26. Words on Walls

The pages of high-end decorating magazines are filled with pictures of walls that talk. The walls don't literally speak, of course. Instead, they display favorite folk sayings, bits of poetry, or quotes from famous and infamous people throughout history.

If you have a favorite saying, you're ready to get to work. If not, spend some quality time with books of quotations, such as The Oxford Book of Quotations, Bartlett's Famous Quotes and The Quotable Woman. These books are filled with interesting, inspirational quotes from a wide variety of sources. So, too, are Internet sites that feature quotations. Type "famous quotations" into a search engine and browse until you find something that inspires or amuses you. You're likely to live with these words for a while, so be sure to choose something that reflects your personality and interests or your sense of humor.

One key to a project like this is making the words proportional to the space where they're displayed, and that can take some trial and error. (This is where patience comes in handy.) If you're working with a soffit or other small linear space, try making the letters about two-thirds the height of the soffit. You may prefer to have the words larger or smaller, but two-thirds is a good starting point.

The font you choose should fit the room as well as the saying. A casual font with a little attitude works well for a short, funny saying. Flowing script sets the tone for poetry or sentimental thoughts. Extremely complex fonts are difficult to work with and difficult to read, so it's often best to avoid them.

Tools & Materials ▸

Laser or carpenter's level
Stylus or dull pencil
Graphite paper
Artist's paintbrushes
Craft paint
Craft paint in a slightly darker color (optional)

How to Paint Words on Walls

1

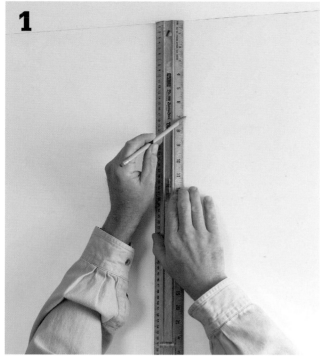

Measure the available space and evaluate the quotations you're considering. Imagine where you would break the lines and how you want the words stacked or displayed.

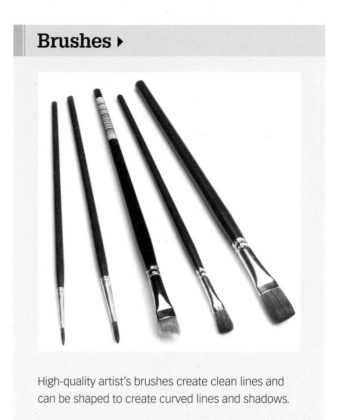

High-quality artist's brushes create clean lines and can be shaped to create curved lines and shadows.

2

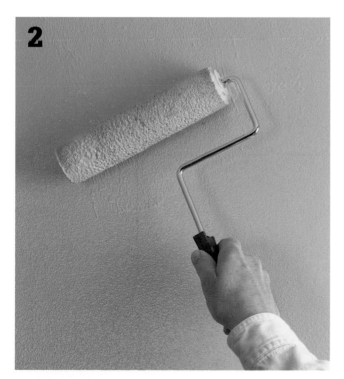

If necessary, fill any holes or dents in the wall and repair any cracks. Prime and paint the wall with two coats of eggshell or flat latex paint.

3

On a computer, select a font and size, and create a design for the words. Refer to the wall measurements taken in Step 1, and arrange the words of the quotation to fit.

(continued)

4

Print out the quotation and trim away the edges of the paper. Tape the printouts on the wall and evaluate the size and placement of the words. Keep trying sizes and arrangements until you're satisfied.

5

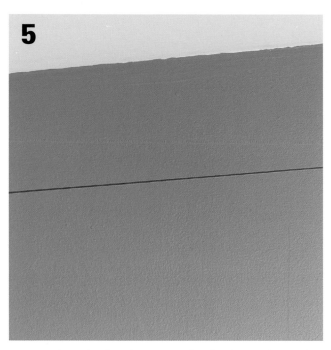

Set up a laser level to shoot a baseline for the words onto the wall. If you don't have a laser level, use a carpenter's level or a bubblestick and a pencil to create a faint line.

6

Hold a piece of graphite paper against the wall, and tape the printout over it. (Be sure you're using graphite paper, not carbon paper. It doesn't smudge.) Line up the base of the letters with the laser line or pencil guideline.

7

Trace the words, using a stylus or other blunt tool with a blunt end. The goal is to create a pattern line without tearing the printout or the graphite paper. Remove the printouts and graphite paper and check the pattern lines. Fill out any faint lines or skipped areas with a pencil.

8

Pour a small puddle of the lighter paint color onto a plastic palette. Dampen an angled paintbrush with water and pat it on a clean paper towel. Dip the corner of the long side of the brush into the craft paint and draw it across the palette to get the paint flowing smoothly.

9

Paint the large, straight, open areas of the letters. Wash out the brush in plain water about every other time you load it, and continue to load only the long side of the brush with paint. If you have to stop in the middle of the project, wash out the brush with soap and water and reshape it before it dries.

10

Use a round-tip brush to paint the curved portions of the letters. Dampen the brush and load only one side with paint. Pull the brush across the palette to distribute the paint evenly, as you did with the angled brush. Draw the brush along the pencil lines, pushing down slightly more as you sweep around curves. The brush should flow along the curves and leave graceful, accurate lines.

Variation ▶

Wash the palette and the angled brush. Pour a small puddle of the darker paint onto the palette and load one side of the damp brush with it. Stroke the brush across the palette until the paint blends with the water on the brush and runs from dark on the long side of the brush to light on the other side. Lightly sweep the brush around the inside edges and curves of the letters, creating a slight shadow.

27. Aged Finish

An aged finish confers instant character on any piece of furniture. With not much more than a wave of your magic paintbrush, you can transform an ordinary new piece of furniture into a treasure that appears to have been part of the family for generations.

The actual process of aging a finish is quite simple, but doing it well takes some planning and a little imagination. Before starting a project, look at the piece carefully and think about how it is used and which areas would show wear if it actually were old. Generally speaking, wear first appears in the areas where a piece is touched often—behind or around handles, on the edges, at the backs of seats, and in the center of the top front rung of a chair. These are the areas you should plan to distress.

Tools & Materials ▸

Cordless screwdriver	Small can of water-
2" synthetic-bristle	based wood stain
brush	Furniture wax
1½" synthetic-bristle	Flat-finish latex paint
brush	in a dark color
Putty knife	Flat-finish latex paint
Extra-fine sandpaper	in lighter color
Tack cloth	Satin-finish
Soft cotton rags	polyurethane spray

Vintage pieces typically show wear in the places where they've been handled for generations. Distressing the paint in these areas creates an authentic looking aged finish.

How to Create an Aged Finish

Take out any drawers. Carefully remove all the hardware from the piece. Most drawer handles have a screw (or two) on the inside face of the drawer. Remove the screws and pull off the handles. When removing hinges, support the door as you remove the screws.

Lightly sand the surface with fine-grit sandpaper. Sand—in the direction of the grain—until the surface is smooth and even. Remove the sanding dust with tack cloth.

Stain the entire piece with dark water-based stain, such as walnut or dark oak. Wipe on an even coat of stain, using a brush or clean cloth. Let the stain penetrate the wood for about one minute, and then wipe off the excess with a clean, dry cloth. Let the stain dry for at least four hours.

Apply furniture wax to the areas you want to distress, such as the edges and under any handles. Draw a quick sketch of the piece and mark the areas where you have applied the wax.

(continued)

Apply the lighter paint color over one side of the piece, painting with the grain of the wood. (Paint only one side at a time, because the paint must be wet for the next step.)

Working quickly, apply the darker paint color to the same side of the piece, blending the darker paint into the lighter shade. Continue painting one side at a time until the whole piece is painted. Let the paint dry at least 40 minutes, but no longer than an hour.

Scrape the paint off the areas where you applied furniture wax, using a putty knife. (If you don't remember exactly where you applied the wax, refer to the diagram you made in Step 4.)

Use fine-grit sandpaper to smooth any rough spots created by the putty knife. Let the piece dry completely.

9

Spray a coat of polyurethane finish on the entire piece and let it dry. Apply a second coat and let it dry.

10

When the finish is completely dry, replace the hardware.

Variation ▶

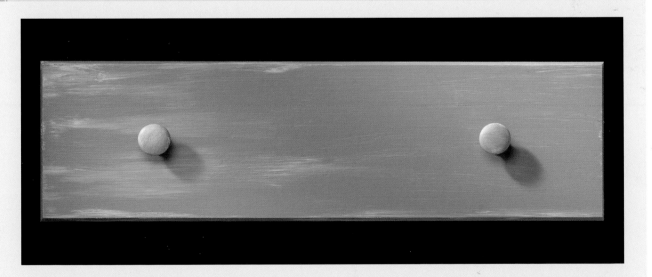

If you want paint rather than stain to show in the distressed areas, paint the entire piece and let it dry. Next, apply furniture wax to selected areas and then add the two paint colors and let them dry. Sand away the paint over the waxed areas, being careful to sand only down to the first paint color.

28. Pickled Paint

Pickling is a simple effect created by painting the piece with watered-down paint and then removing the excess. The most important thing to remember when using this technique is to work quickly—the paint must still be wet as you wipe it away.

Pieces made of pine are good choices for this technique. Because it's very porous, pine absorbs the paint quickly, and plenty of color is left after the excess has been wiped away. Other softwoods will also work, but pieces made of hardwoods, such as oak, aren't good candidates for a pickled finish.

Tools & Materials ▸

Cordless screwdriver
Fine-grit sandpaper
Tack cloth
2" small natural
  sponge
Thick white cotton rag

Flat-finish interior
  latex paint
One quart of water
Satin-finish
  polyurethane
  spray

How to Create a Pickled Finish

Remove drawers from dressers and upholstered seats from chairs. If the piece has hardware, carefully remove it.

Combine one part of paint with three parts of water. Stir the mixture thoroughly.

Paint the paint-and-water mixture onto the piece, using a small sponge. Follow the grain of the wood as you paint, and try to avoid drips and runs. If the piece is large, divide it into sections and complete one section before painting another.

Using a thick cotton rag, wipe excess paint off the piece. Work quickly, because the paint must be wet in order to be successfully removed.

Spray on a light coat of polyurethane finish and let it dry for an hour. Apply a second coat and let the piece dry overnight.

Replace the upholstered seat or hardware.

Pickling Variation ▶

For pieces made of hardwoods or to create a more traditional look for a formal room, you can achieve a pickled effect with stain rather than paint. Select a water-based stain in a color of your choice.

Prepare the piece by removing any hardware and sanding the surface lightly (see page 91). Combine one part of stain with three parts of water and stir thoroughly.

Use a small sponge brush to apply the stain-water mixture, following the grain of the wood. While the mixture is still wet, wipe away any excess. Allow the piece to dry, then apply two coats of polyurethane spray (see pages 91 to 92). When the polyurethane is dry, replace the hardware as necessary.

If desired, change the fabric on the seat before replacing it. Pry up the staples and remove the old fabric. Use the old fabric as a pattern to cut a new piece.

Place the fabric upside down on a worktable. Wrap the fabric to the back of the seat and tape it in place. Turn the seat over and check the positioning of the fabric; adjust as necessary. Turn the seat back over and staple the fabric to the seat, placing a staple about every inch along the perimeter of the seat.

Use a spinner tool to remove paint and solvent. Wash the roller cover or brush with solvent, then attach it to the spinner. Pumping the handle throws liquids out of the roller cover or brush. Hold the spinner inside a cardboard box or 5-gallon bucket to catch paint and avoid splatters.

29. Cleanup

At the end of a paint job you may choose to throw away the roller covers, but the paint pans, roller handles, and brushes can be cleaned and stored for future use. Stray paint drips can be wiped away if they are still wet. A putty knife or razor will remove many dried paint spots on hardwood or glass. Remove stubborn paint from most surfaces with a chemical cleaner.

Cleaning products include (from left): chemical cleaner, spinner tool, cleaner tool for brushes and roller covers.

Cleanup Tips ▸

Comb brush bristles with the spiked side of a cleaner tool. This aligns the bristles so they dry properly.

Scrape paint from a roller cover with the curved side of cleaner tool. Remove as much paint as possible before washing the tools with solvent.

Store brushes in their original wrappers, or fold the bristles inside brown wrapping paper. Store washed roller covers on end to avoid flattening the nap.

Remove dried splatters with a chemical cleaner. Before using cleaner, test an inconspicuous area to make sure the surface is colorfast.

Creative Publishing international

Copyright © 2011
Creative Publishing international, Inc.
400 First Avenue North, Suite 300
Minneapolis, Minnesota 55401
1-800-328-0590
www.creativepub.com
All rights reserved

Printed in China

10 9 8 7 6 5 4 3 2 1

Here's How Painting
Created by: The Editors of Creative Publishing international, Inc., in cooperation with Black & Decker. Black & Decker® is a trademark of The Black & Decker Corporation and is used under license.

President/CEO: Ken Fund

Home Improvement Group

Publisher: Bryan Trandem
Managing Editor: Tracy Stanley
Senior Editor: Mark Johanson

Creative Director: Michele Lanci-Altomare
Art Direction/Design: Jon Simpson, Brad Springer, James Kegley

Lead Photographer: Joel Schnell

Production Managers: Laura Hokkanen, Linda Halls

Page Layout Artist: Kim Winscher